THE SUN,
THE MOON
& RIPE
CUCUMBERS

PREVIOUSLY BY THE AUTHOR

Voices from Another Room (Crane River)

THE SUN, THE MOON & RIPE CUCUMBERS

༄

NEW POEMS

༄

Stuart Payne

CRANE RIVER
Cape Town, 2025

ACKNOWLEDGEMENTS

'Words for Dia!kwain' won *New Contrast*'s 2022 National Poetry Prize. Some of the poems here collected first appeared in *Botsotso, New Contrast, Stanzas* and on the AVBOB Poetry Competition website. 'For Whom There is No Grief' was commissioned by and appeared in the AVBOB Poetry Competition anthology, *I wish I'd said…* Vol. 2.

ISBN 978-1-0370-1686-8
© This compilation, Crane River 2025
© Individual poems, Stuart Payne 2025
All rights reserved. No part of this publication may be reproduced, stored in a retrieval system, or transmitted by any form whatsoever without the prior permission of the author or the publisher.

Editor & Publisher	Crane River
Layout & typesetting	User Friendly
Distribution	uHlanga Press
Proofed by	Keith Edwards
Cover art	'Cucumber with leaf and flowers isolated on white' Romiri77 (Dreamstime.com)
Cover design	uHlanga Press
Author photograph	Lynne Payne
Typeset in	Adobe Garamond Pro 11.5 on 14 pt

I'd like to thank Crane River for their continued support and skilful editing, and Jo-Anne Friedlander for her layout of this book. Thank you to Colin, Dianne, and Lilly. Welcome to Naira! Thank you to Gus Ferguson and Hugh Hodge (posthumously), and Sarah Ruden for their early encouragement, and to Finuala Dowling, Elisa Galgut and Archie Swanson for their support. Thank you to Geoffrey Haresnape and Patricia Schonstein for their readings. Thank you, of course, to my parents, to whom the book is dedicated. And thank you to my grandparents – Reg and Winnie, Cedric and Molly, about whom I've tried to write on many occasions.

CONTENTS

Oh, I Wrote a Few Lines ... 8

I Where Will We Go?

Wilderness	11
Bioluminescence	12
Wakening	13
Under Saturn	14
This Garden	15
Grass and Earth	17
Rain Delay, 1982	18
After Héloïse, c.1130 CE	19
Play Us a Song	20
The Planet	21
About a Bay	23
Memories: A Chant	24
The House on the Hill	25
After Aias	26

II Oceans of the Moon

After the Funeral	29
Oceans of the Moon	30
Sanctity	31
Hour	32
Another World	33
Among the Dead	34
To Wake the Dead	35
Elegy 8	36
Elegy 9	37
Ghost	38

III Birds in Ancient Paintings

On Cats	41
Indian Hawthorn	44

For Whom There is No Grief	45
Photograph	47
Painting	48
Flutter and Coo	49
The Killing Schedule	51
Dogs are Playing	52

IV Qurtuba

Words for Dia!kwain	55
Qurtuba	58
Euterpe	59
Exodus	60
On a Persian Miniature	62

V The Sun, the Moon & Ripe Cucumbers

Diocletian	67
Nocturne	68
Conversations in a Time of Isolation	69
A Comedy Tonight	71
Across the Hills to Home	72
Encounters	73
Babylonian Thought	74
Cucumbers	75
Mulberry	76
Supermarket Fruit Pot	77
To Attar's Nightingale	78
Tourist Bus, Long Street	79
Ducks in a Garden, Cape Town	80
Revolutions	81
Into Town	82
Notes on the poems	84
Notes on the author	86

to my father
Keith Attwood Payne
(1946–2021)
and my mother
Lynne

with love

Oh, I Wrote a Few Lines

For the lonely and lost and in pain,
for the hopeless and soon to be slain,
for the sick and the sad and insane,
oh, I wrote a few lines.

They're not words that will banish their fear
or the sorrow for all they held dear,
perhaps they're not words they will hear,
but I wrote a few lines

where we'll be together again
with the spirits of those we knew then,
although they're beyond mortal ken
and it's just a few lines

and only a small thing to give
and soon we must leave them and live,
so I'm hoping that you will forgive
that it's just a few lines.

I

Where Will We Go?

The universe is true for all of us and dissimilar to each of us.
MARCEL PROUST

Wilderness

> People who accuse us of putting in too much violence,
> [should see] what we leave on the cutting-room floor.
> DAVID ATTENBOROUGH

We separate the trash these days,
and use a well-point on the garden,
planted now for birds and insects
flitting through the changeful air.

We read of ice collapsed in waves
and turn lights off when not in use;
we take tote bags when going shopping.
All the usual things you do.

But there are times, observing nature's
ways, I'd sooner pave it all
and end these rounds of life and death
in something pleasant, like a plaza.

Birds would fly, or forms of birds,
as if their golden feathers felt
the winds, and marble beasts would pace
the land below, their eyes of jewels.

Lions would roar, like blood still flowed,
but drinking deer not start in fright,
and whales would rise from burnished oceans,
ageless under wheeling skies.

Bioluminescence

Cumulus clouds,
bright with city lights,
are spread across the sky beyond the curtains
parted for a moment by a child's hand:
saffron clouds, like living beings
drifting in their native habitat,
expanding and diminishing with breath
or with their will, their presence changing streets
to ocean floors or unfamiliar plains,
as worries formed in quiet homes disperse
and life on earth is understood again
beneath the peaceful glow of other lives
subsisting on the currents of the sky
or, more than that, like blessings of the gods,
gathering the earth within their care,
reminding those below that daily life
is not forgotten,
nor beyond their plans.

The clouds drift slowly by,
covering the sky beyond the curtains,
luminous with lights of streets and homes
where life's observed
and understanding's
altered by their purpose.

Wakening

She'll dream of happiness again tonight
where once she would have dreamt of tangled things:
their clutching grasp now drugged to feebleness,
she's free to drift with one she loves,
or yet another,
being young again,
with those she knew and others,
real as them,
passing through a vivid world
whose strangeness only shows in its departure.

She dwells a moment more,
half in joy and half in loss
before the warmth of touch quite disappears
and then must wake to ghosts and fearfulness
and to a body none has ever held.

Under Saturn

I see us in a vernal land
where seedless flowers bud and bloom
round guard-less towns, where generations
pass untroubled by the tomb,
where untilled fields give up their fruit
and oak trees flow with honey.

And there, where Saturn has returned
and orders live in harmony,
where wolves lap streams by careless flocks
I'd live with you as we would be,
where untilled fields give up their fruit
and oak trees flow with honey.

This Garden

How long has this been land,
and been *this* land,
scattered here across millennia
from circling seas?

I'm digging down
through several layers of earth,
dark and sandy pale,
to plant a coral tree.

I balance it in place,
shovelling back the earth
now mixed with compost.

Still, the land remains.

I wash my hands,
watching granules spiralling the drain.

The land remains,
as through the centuries
since waves withdrew,
and shrubs and flowers rose,
decaying into soil,
and animals, some strange,
made this their home.

At least since then,
when people travelled
down the continent to find this plain,

altering the land
where they would lie –
we know of hearths
and walls of ochre art.

It still remained this land,
and they were *here*,
where now I tend my plants,
feeling sandy earth beneath their feet
in fields of drifting sedge
and silver shrubs
and fragrant bushes,
called by vanished names.

Grass and Earth

Who'll know the smell of this grass and earth
or feel these winds from what I write
of them? What words tell these things?
Our language has been shaped by sight
and sound, and though I call them 'rich'
or 'fresh', what is it that I mean?
You'll understand me differently;
we have no categories like *green*
for telling this – to call you here
to smell the compost laid on sand,
or know the movements of the grass
of this, instead of other, land
where roots descend and tiny creatures
crawl – to feel the soft winds blow,
and know the smell of this grass and earth
and rest where words have yet to go.

Rain Delay, 1982

Dimly, players cross the TV screen,
dissolving in a haze of faded film
as hollow sounds of rackets and applause
emerge in a suburban living room.

The television flickers as they run,
chasing tennis balls already lost
amid the grass, as in a distant past
glimpsed obscurely in a scrying glass.

After Héloïse, c.1130 CE

Still I love and yet must hope for nothing.

Though I flee the world we knew, I find
I can't renounce the one I love – I love,
for neither vows nor convent still my heart.
I've not been turned to marble, resting here
forgetful of my loss in cloistered quiet,
gazing from my niche on centuries
to calm the souls of those who pass before me.

Tell me as a lover to submit
to your commands – let me feel your hand
relieve their weight – tell me of the blessings
that they bring and solitude will not
appear so dreadful. Hearts once moved like mine
are not soon made serene but fluctuate
instead from love to hate before, at last,
they reach tranquillity.

                      Your songs proclaimed
our joy through many lands; is it not right
to speak of this new joy? Teach me
in the ways of heaven's love. Speak to me,
so by your guidance I might live without you.

Play Us a Song

Pick up your instruments, play us a song
with lyrics of love and clashing guitars
– as if to waken the gods from their sleep –
and take us away with a handful of bars
as bottles are emptied. The night has been long
but pick up your instruments, play us a song

and sing us a melody louder than doubt,
with clattering rhythms, so we might believe
that all that is lost could be gathered again
in your raggedy art, though soon we must leave
as windows grow pale. The night has been long,
so pick up your instruments, play us a song.

The Planet

> 'Tis a strange place, this Limbo!
> 'Limbo', SAMUEL TAYLOR COLERIDGE

A strange place, this planet,
orbiting a small and distant sun,
stripped of atmosphere
by solar winds
or some catastrophe
as yet unstudied.

And who is there to study it
and call it a catastrophe?

The undulating plains, the mountain spires,
are bare of life; the unprotected surface,
pocked with craters,
unobserved, with none to hear the muted fall
of rock and metal shattering the land,
with clouds of dust erupting
to the bright, unblinking stars.

At times a storm will rise,
not cold, not hot,
more cold than hot
if there were life to judge,
and all the sky's obscured,
the land abraded.

But there may come a day a module lands,
an unseen flash of light across the sky

that settles on the still primeval dust
and watchful beings move across the planet,
guarded from the barrenness and storms
by suits and shelter
shaped by ages' knowledge.

They may come upon twin needle peaks
and see bright galaxies between their heights,
and watch the light of stars
on ancient cliffs and trackless plains,
or reach a crater's edge
and raise their faces to a golden sky
to feel the sunlight of another noon,
as in those early hours
of the planet,
they look on it
and call it beautiful.

About a Bay

I wrote this place for you when you need rest,
where you can paddle in a long, white bay
and watch the waves roll in, as sure as breath,
and hear the call of gulls and feel the spray,

or wander hills – I've written rivers there,
with boats that wait to guide you on their flow
through fragrant fields, where gentle breezes stir
as songbirds sing and wildflowers grow.

Oh, life can get on top of you at times
but when you're weary or (please, no) distressed,
these waves will roll to shore and rivers run.
I wrote this place for you when you need rest.

Memories: A Chant

Soon our voices will be silent
and our bodies still, and fade
like hills and gorges, tangled groves,
and grassy fields where we have played
and danced beneath our only sun:
we play, we dance, we will be none.

Though some may dream of heaven's fields
we have no life beyond this day.
Until we feel the light grow faint
and know the moment's come, we play
and dance beneath our only sun:
we play, we dance, we will be none.

The House on the Hill

Who would choose to live in a house like this
but those who've watched the endless plains
and found no life beneath their sun or moon,
no shelter from the heat or sweeping rains?
Who would choose to live in a house like this
but those who've known no other?
                                                On a hill,
as if to watch the plains a little further,
it might appear serene when all is still
but clouds amass and winds begin to moan,
and deep within the hill foundations groan
and we must board the windows, bar the doors
and, through the storm, replace each fallen stone
so winds to come may find no further purchase.

Little's left intact; a house remains,
though who would choose to live in a house like this
but those who've watched the endless plains
and found no grasses reaching to the sun
nor circling birds to tell of death below?
But there's a storm to come and it will fall
and then where will we go? Where will we go?

After Aias

> Slay us at least in the light
> *The Iliad,* Book XVII

I ask you this. No more than this:
that you will let these mists disperse
so I may see the field in light
again, unburdened by your curse,
then, when you know this mortal's measure,
let me fall – that is your pleasure.

It's no favour that I ask.
But let me do what must be done
as others may, not lost in mist
but in the clear light of the sun,
then, when you know this mortal's measure,
let me fall – that is your pleasure.

II

Oceans of the Moon

I have fallen – I fell because it was said that my forefather Rarabe would appear, and my father would appear, and my mother would appear, and that I should not be old.
CHIEF MHALA OF THE NDLAMBE XHOSA

After the Funeral

The sky is blue beyond the sliding doors
with tufts of clouds dispersing as they pass
above the chattering world, as on the days
we'd go to Fish Hoek beach and Dad would take us

diving off the rocks to swim with goggles
over sunlit sand and shoals of tiny
fish would flicker by, or days he'd spend,
when still a boy, with friends along a river's

marshy banks as fat platanna watched
from shallow pools and life held secrets yet
to be explored amid the rustling reeds,
with parents waiting at adventure's end,

or days when children laugh again outside
and hurry on, excited by the life
that lies ahead, as tufts of clouds disperse
and there's no one to tell them what there was.

Oceans of the Moon

Perhaps I'll find the words to raise the past
at will, to conjure it in careful lines
as in a tale an invocation's cast
to form a vision where a seer divines

some distant knowledge – words exactly phrased
so they, like flower scents, will let me roam
amid the vanished world that they have raised,
in summer days you slowly paddled home.

And yet, what spell would let you roam with me?
Though I move in vanished days with you,
your ghost is still. The apparitions flee
and we are lost like everything you knew,
no more to wade some shallow, warm lagoon
than swim across the oceans of the moon.

Sanctity

As we meet, we're saying our goodbyes;
we see the ruin of our holy places,
hoping that beyond our mortal eyes
a heaven waits – that we'll divine some traces
left in nature to confirm our hope
that all we love must have a greater scope,
that far beyond our grasp of time and space,
beyond the faintest star, within each cell,
there is the something other that we chase,
a sphere where gods and those we loved can dwell
from which, at times, escapes a puzzling sign,
a whisper of the life of the divine
to tell us, though these days must soon be through,
I need not fear to say goodbye to you.

Hour

The hour is uncertain – that we know,
and so the hour's unreal, half out of time:
although we might imagine it, although
we choose from sickness, chance or crime,
does one appear more likely than the rest?
And if it does how else might it unfold?
Will you make a last defiant jest
or will you dream, forgetting that you're old?
And yet our deaths will have their certain hours,
when we'll, perhaps, have better things to do,
parting us from all that had been ours,
and all who loved us from the lives they knew.

Another World

Another world was lost tonight,
another mind through which we passed
in memory and hope. It's lost,
and we had hoped that it would last
a little more than this, at least.
But all we were to her is gone,
while all she was to us remains
with us – and so we carry on
in rooms she knew, in preparation,
thankful that our lives had crossed.
And yet a world was lost tonight
and she remains and we are lost.

Among the Dead

Our days are spent among the dead:
they come to us in memories
of lives that passed though days like these
with us, or rise from pages read;

we trace their ancient artistry
to tell us of the world they knew
or delve the earth to bring to view
a citadel or vanished sea

and populate the world with ghosts.
If they've no life beyond our thought,
if breaths once drawn and struggles fought
by tiny lives and splendid hosts

must disappear with us again,
we recognise their lives in ours
and in ourselves preserve the hours
we knew with others living then,

or brush a spirit's trailing hem
who moves in centuries long fled.
Our days are spent among the dead;
our place will be with them.

To Wake the Dead

We'll sing to those who cannot hear,
or if they hear we cannot know;
we'll sing to them and tears will flow
for all we held and still hold dear

and all that we must still forget,
but in the middle of our song
imagine those for whom we long
have heard us though they're sleeping yet.

They hear, they wake, they rise again
to move among us as we play.
Stay, my loves – they cannot stay
and life can't be as it was then.

Too soon the notes no longer play,
and we must take ourselves to bed
to sleep as if among the dead
then wake to meet a silent day.

Elegy 8

Goodbye, my small, grey cat, my watchful cat
who found the house and chose us for your own,
and played with other cats on morning walks,
and in the halls at night when we were young.

Goodbye, my small, grey cat, who travelled here
with damaged teeth and allergies to treat,
to rest in safety, curled beneath your blankets,
flexing paws as trusted steps approached

or dropping lightly to the porch's floor
amid your catnip mice. A world remained,
though years and lives went by, an understanding
in your feline mind as you observed us,

sunk in winter's ruff or stretching in the warmth
of summer suns. You chose us for your own
and you were happy – let me think of that.
Goodbye, my small, grey cat, my watchful cat.

Elegy 9

Go in peace, my love, where friends have gone,
both solemn-eyed and playful. Go in peace,
where there's no weariness – but let me keep
a place for you with me, held in words

that you'd not understand, no more than they
could draw decay from flesh, or bring you back,
young and thrilled by all the world contained
and dancing round the paws of patient elders.

Let me see you, tall and courteous
and welcoming to all, both cats and people.
'Highly strung,' the locum said in truth,
but pleased to share the comforts of your life,

and then (there is no other word) a wife
appeared, following the path of friends
to settle here, calming fragile nerves
and curling with you (only her) in sleep -

and let me see the final days again,
when we would find the sun, as weavers sang,
and you and she would rest, as I sat near,
in places that you'd known since you were young,

through years I'd hear a rustle in the leaves
as, tiger-bright, an eager face appeared;
as if you might emerge yet through these words
and curl about my legs in courtly welcome.

Ghost

I left a ghost for you beside the window
so you'd not be alone when you came home.
I left a little ghost for each of you.
and parts of me remain where spirits roam.

III

Birds in Ancient Paintings

When I play with my cat, how do I know
that she is not passing time with me rather than I with her?
MICHEL DE MONTAIGNE

III

Birds in Ancient Palestine

On Cats

Here I lie, reluctantly at rest,
as analgesics go about their work.
The cats are resting – tranquilly, I think:
one beneath a bush within the garden
fenced for their protection; one in bed
beneath a table, lying with a friend;
and one luxuriating in the porch's
warmth, living through their history,
through minds and senses shaped by centuries
of trial and travel, small ancestral creatures
crossing vanished plains and back again
to find the grain and mice of fertile lands.

And there, in cultivation, something changed.
Something over mice and raided grain –
it isn't pleasant – I wish mice no harm –
but *lybica* accepted partnership
(of all the many, *lybica* alone!)
and supple figures padded through the stores,
travelling trading routes, the bane of rodents,
nurtured and then altered by affection,
sometimes fleeing vilest superstition,
changing human customs as they lived
through centuries' companionship and work,
their paw prints on the pages of our past.

Their senses are unaltered, so I read,
from those of cats that first approached the stores,
and resting in this afternoon they rest
within a world as strange to me as it

is known. Developed since our final common
ancestor (who scurried through the grasses
and the forests of a world remade,
scenting air for predators and prey)
their noses know a life of subtle change,
distinguishing a myriad of smells
to form their worlds; their eyes, evolved to judge
positions in the night, omit the depth
of colours I observe; and when I shift
to see her in the sun, her eyes half-closed,
she turns her ears towards me, shuts her eyes
and opens them again as autumn drifts
across her curling whiskers, placing her
within her feline space. I murmur words
and rise and hobble off to see the others.

He's still asleep in bed beneath the table,
resting with his friend, and on the porch
she's stretching in the sun. They flex their paws
and sink into their dreams, like forebears resting,
waiting for the business of the night.

(Continued after some weeks)

This long, large cat, so often on his nerves,
now moves with gentle breath;
his snowy friend, who rollicked down the garden
for his meal, is resting, full and sleepy
by his side; and on the porch she's stretched
across her toys, the eldest now where once
she was the youngest. The brother of the friend,
with solemn eyes, once greeted her with mutual
dignity and I would place him here,

like many more who moved within the safety
of these rooms, where medicines will aid
a hobbled back and treat the allergies
of small, grey cats.

                Something will remain,
though held in words that they'll not understand,
no more than I will understand their memories,
or so I read. What do you dream?
What knowledge lies within familiar lives,
with habits formed in days before we met,
with siblings sightless in your mothers' warmth,
or learning of the world beyond her care?
They rest, untouched by human questioning,
to wake again to be as they were made,
like birds in ancient paintings, singing still,
or monarchs rendered by the scholar's quill.

Indian Hawthorn

The bees are buzzing in the flowers
as she dozes where she sits,
half beyond the passing hours,
soothed by busy humming. It's
the height of spring and on a breeze
there drifts the scent that calls the bees,

though what antennae might perceive,
must be quite other than she knows,
like their lenses, as they weave
amid a world that never shows
itself to her. How strange it seems.
The bees are busy as she dreams.

For Whom There is No Grief

I grieve for those for whom there is no grief,
though it brings no comfort or relief

to them and little happiness to me.
But there it is. Because they were as we

are now? They were alive and now are not,
and we will soon be held by urn or plot

or scattered to the winds. Perhaps that's so,
or partly so, but what a snake might know

and see and feel through serpent's eyes and skin
must be so unalike, so un-akin

to human life there might seem little room
for empathy despite the common doom.

Did I say snake? Moles, then, or ducks – all things
that fear or are content; things on wings

and paws and fins; things that kill each other;
things for which I would have had another

end: all for which there is no grief,
no graveside tears or comforting belief

in afterlives, both cats and humans left
alone without concern, none left bereft.

I grieve for those for whom there is no grief,
because it brings no comfort or relief,

because I cannot call on them to rise,
to rise and breach the walls of paradise.

Photograph

A child lies sleeping in his denim outfit,
slumped across a pouf.
                        Behind him sits
a small, dark tabby cat, crouched to watch
an early Auckland dusk through sliding doors.

Click.

      The tabby hears her people move.
The camera's put away, the boy's picked up,
perhaps, and carried down the corridor
to bed… Later she may slip outside

to prowl among the roses and the reeds
and feel the air she knows across her fur
in moments never caught by photographs
or touched by thoughts of changes yet to come.

Painting

I should have been a painter, as I hoped.
I'd paint the three of you: a black-and-white
bull terrier, a white bull terrier,
a golden torbie. Paint you as motifs,
appearing in the midst of foliage,
as in the midst of thoughts, with rodents, birds
and tortoises in deathless happiness,
or paint you to the life – I'd paint the beach
where you, my kindly friend, warned off a dog
you judged too wild for me; or trace how you,
my brother's gentle pet, removed the only
pear that tree has grown. And you, our cat,
adventurer when young, I'd drape you safely
round my mother's neck, as you and she
appeared outside the lounge. Shaded lamps
and TV ads would glow across the scene:
the dogs relaxing by their panels' warmth
as I lay on my couch, my brother his,
and Dad would be there, home and in his chair,
as faces turned to you, and you went in.

Flutter and Coo

Doves and pigeons
walk into the laundry
now and then,
when nobody's around,
bobbing on in curiosity,
or simply lack of worry,
through the stillness,
noting our appliances
with dark, bright eyes
until they're stopped,
trapped by sliding doors,
and flutter in sudden confusion,
then in panic
as we near,
with safety just beyond
the baffling glass,
some cooing in self-comfort
as we snatch them,
some as if enraged
and others still,
their small hearts racing
under soft,
warm feathers.

Each of them is different
as we take them to the open door
and toss them free
to feel the sun and wind
and hang there,
fleetingly,

as if amazed,
then beat their wings
towards the rippling trees.

The Killing Schedule

I die untouched by gentle thoughts
of those who would condemn this end,
the strangeness of this earth-less place
in which our lives are penned.

I remember gentle flanks,
and smells of food and life I knew
but I've no words or wish to pass
those memories to you,

nor can I know that all that was
was other than it seemed to me
and led me to this earth-less place
and all that's yet to be.

But still I feel and still I fear
and still we're made to trudge along
this path to ends I cannot know
but that I know are wrong,

through smells of blood and cleanliness
and sounds no creature ever made
and wary calls of sheep and shouts
of men and I'm afraid.

My body swings, my body shakes,
my life is yours – is hers, is his –
in this, a world that shouldn't be
and mustn't be and is.

Dogs are Playing

Dogs are playing on the mountainside,
two dogs and children in a forest stream
that ripples down from pool to rocky pool,
parting leaves to pass as in a dream
to other clearings, called by sounds and smells
of forest life and by adventures read
in shared and yet diverse experience
to travel on and know what lies ahead,
as in a dream we pass to other worlds,
accepting the reality of all
we meet, beguiled by their strangeness though
we are: uncertain of what might befall,
we reach a forest glade – a secret lair –
turning stones to see what's hidden there,
listening to the calls of forest birds,
bright and piercing in the humid air
as water ripples coolly round our feet
towards the sea, far from where it rose
in mountain depths, tannin-stained yet sweet,
with much to tell a snuffling canine nose.
But what was told; what adventures known?
Like children's tales of which you weren't aware,
mingling words with waterfalls and leaves,
but which, to be, required your presence there
and if I found my way back there today,
and dreamt again of all that there might be
along the stream, beyond un-parted leaves,
what would I dream but you were there with me?

IV

Qurtuba

The only true voyage of discovery, the only fountain of Eternal Youth, would be not to visit strange lands but to possess other eyes, to behold the universe through the eyes of another, of a hundred others, to behold the hundred universes that each of them beholds,
that each of them is.
MARCEL PROUST

Words for Dia!kwain

> And we perceived a thing which looked like
> a little child as it sat upon the (salt) pan
> 'Concerning Apparitions', DIA!KWAIN

Something will remain to mark the loss,
gathered here, far from all we knew,
and guarded in this village by the sea,
the songs of lands where I was born and grew

and killed – yes, killed, and it was self-defence;
the judge knew it was so when I was brought
before him, following the journey south
from where we sang, where in my life we caught

the water-bull and rain fell where we willed,
where still when rains return the fields bloom
with many colours and fill the air with smells
like honey, far, so far from this, my room

beneath the mountains. I must leave
and look for those I knew while I have breath.
My chest is growing weak and I should stay,
I'm told. But even in this village death

will come. It found him here, the friend who wrote
my tales. Now it's found another friend –
the letter came to us some days ago.
He knew the past and soon there'll be an end

to stories told and our shamanic dreams.
I want to find my family and the songs
where they survive amid the grass and bush,
somewhere in the land while it belongs

to them, and they to it, and where our language
will remain the medium of life
a little longer. I have no illusions.
There'll be no moderation of the strife

between the peoples and we cannot win.
When commandos came, we felt our blood
turn into smoke, a smoke surrounding us,
in which we fought… but I have seen it flood

the ground when they departed. I've heard the guns
and seen the fences, seen the foreign herds.
There's not the blood remaining in our clans
to guard us from the future. I leave my words

with you who learnt my language, with you – her sister
and his wife – your children, and this place,
this oak-lined street, this portion of that city
by the sea, the ruin of my race.

A world is lost and yet the words will keep
a glimpse of our existence at its end.
Is that not so? They will be understood.
Or is it on our world that they depend

for understanding? But there's no time for more
and you who mourn will understand my need
for what I've lost. I'll travel to Calvinia,
then follow news and rumours where they lead

and hope to find my children, somewhere under
speaking stars, where we'll have much to sing;
they'll tell of life across that arid land
and listen to the stories that I bring

of you, and in the spring, we'll feast on corms
of wildflowers. Today it's time to go
but I may come again, bringing tales
I've found so in the future people know

what has been lost. No longer in their language,
something in the stories will survive.
They'll reappear in unfamiliar forms,
the ghosts of a tradition once alive.

Qurtuba

At times, I'd make my way to Cordoba
(or Qurtuba, as it might be), the *taifa*
left unconquered, or the Caliphate
unfallen. Worshippers would kneel amid

the columns of the mosque, the library
would hold its volumes, too, with further knowledge
gained in further years, as students came
from lands of other faiths to learn its wisdom.

I wouldn't change the city that it is,
you understand, just give the slip to time
(no more than that) and live a double day
with people risen from another history.

I'd travel to Byzantium, its walls
un-breached, and it the lord of spacious lands
and seas, as Cordoba would look across
the straits to see Tangiers still held the south.

And in Byzantium the priests would chant,
and incense burn, and voices rise as one
towards the dome, towards the glowing windows,
rising to the promise of the heavens.

Euterpe

> I am a tombstone, an image. Seikilos placed me here
> as a long-lasting sign of deathless remembrance.
> (Seikilos to Euterpe)

The melody plays, rippling through its ancient
scale, as chiselled on the chosen stone
and settled in a graveyard of a city
rich with Roman trade and fruitful fields,

as if the stone still stood beneath the sun
and mournful figures passed among the tombs,
and columns marked with names, and bright reliefs
that told the world *they lived and they were loved.*

Exodus

Though ears of barley rise from fertile fields
as in a dream once dreamt in arid lands,
when fire shimmered on the desert sands
and people spoke of hopes beyond their years;
though sparkling water falls to rocky pools
to splash in bowls in workers' stone-walled homes
and children grow to know ancestral lands,
the thoughts of evening turn to those forbidden
them, who made a mausoleum of sands
more sacred than the art of generations
raising stones on consecrated earth,
and though the stores grow full with wine and grain
and precious oils and folds of flax and wool,
they have no tongues to taste, no flesh to touch,
nor ears to hear the lowing of the herds
at close of day.

                    Would they have been content
if they had lived, the loved ones whom I buried
where they died? Or would they judge this still
too dearly gained, and find a journey's dreams
must dissipate in life as it is lived,
with worries that our labour seeks to still
as seasons pass and able bodies tire
and generations spread across a land
surrounded by the strength of many nations?

Evening's sun is gold across the town,
high upon its hill, as workers wander
home through growing dusk, and tufts of smoke

emerge from homesteads, neat amid the vines
and fields of wheat, where others might have lived
and grown in strength, untroubled by their dreams,
to gaze across the riches of this land
and rest beneath the terebinth and oak.

On a Persian Miniature

> Yusuf and Zulaikha appear in the Bible as Joseph and
> Potiphar's wife and in the Quran as Yusuf and the
> wife of al-Aziz. She is named Zulaikha in later Jewish
> commentary, and in some Muslim traditions
> becomes a symbol of the soul's longing for God.
>
> *Yusuf tends his flock* has been attributed to the painter
> Muhammadi. It illustrates a passage in the book Yusuf and
> Zulaikha by the poet Jami (1440–1492 CE) and
> comes from a volume commissioned by Prince
> Ibrahim Mirza between 1556 and 1565.

She watches from her ornamented tent,
smiling as he tends his flock below
where grass and flowers run through naked rocks
rising to a flat and golden sky.
No shadows fall on them or ever fell
across these hills where goats graze and play
beneath their master's gentle gaze, resting
by a leafy plane where plump-breasted birds
nest and sing.

          An aged man approaches,
bent beneath a weight of firewood
and like the nurse who still protects her secret
he holds an explanation of the idyll.
The herder's unaware a moment more;
the watcher in the tent retains her dreams
a moment more – an endless moment more –
and then their worlds must be explained again.

The images were painted long ago,
somewhere in a wealthy city, bustling
with the trade of Central Asia, where mosques
with patterned tiles, and palaces and tombs,
rose amid the hubbub of the streets
and spacious gardens trilled with running water;
there a harassed prince might find repose
in contemplating poetry and art.

They tell a story not quite unfamiliar,
an ancient story learnt in holy texts
and told again to children, told by poets,
now less a tale of violence than love
and shaped again in Sufi allegory:
a soul's desire for God as earthly quest,
honoured on the orders of a prince
by skilled calligraphers on leaves of gold.

The tale unfolds in vibrant lines and colours
painted on a page of gold grisaille
where leopards, herons, Chinese clouds, a dragon,
twine with vegetation, all in rhythm
with the tale that spills beyond its frame:
a horse's rump, coloured flowers curve
against the monochrome, as if they were
a vision granted us, and for a moment
borders might dissolve and what we glimpse
of shapes and colours be more real to us
than rooms where brushes move with careful strokes,
or streets where sunlight falls and lives go by.

Lines will not converge and we need not
be held in three dimensions, here in this

transfigured world, open to the saints,
where space and time remain in pristine form.

Or so it seems to eyes and mind developed
in another time. Can enough
be gained, enough forgotten – much though we
might read of its tradition – to see the image
as it was to those within the faith,
who decorated mosques' serenity
with arabesques and geometric patterns
and found in them their paradise reflected?
And if a seeing's lost to us, how much
was lost between the brushes' strokes and prince's
observation; between the thought and strokes,
and all who've read the words upon the vision?

The watcher in the tent retains her dreams
a moment more – an endless moment more –
the herder guards his goats a moment more
and understandings pass about their stillness.

V

The Sun, the Moon & Ripe Cucumbers

The fairest thing I leave is the light of the sun,
and the next the bright stars and face of the moon,
and also ripe cucumbers and apples and pears
PRAXILLA

Diocletian

I read of new allegiances,
technologies, and ailing bees
and ask myself what marks an era's
start or end. Might one of these?

What brings an era to completion?
Who predicted Diocletian?

What will others tell of us,
and would we recognise what's told?
Is this the birth of something new
or dying of a world grown old?

What brings an era to completion?
Who predicted Diocletian?

Nocturne

The need for answers wearies the reply.
Give no further thought to mortal plight
but close the page and nod off where you lie;
we'll get no closer to the truth tonight.

Some believe or (doubting that it's true)
dream they make it true in what they write.
Once, perhaps, they'd have enwritten you;
we'll get no closer to the truth tonight,

to reasons they might hide, or not have guessed
and so, with reason, think they have it right,
and judgement might be swayed by lack of rest;
we'll get no closer to the truth tonight.

Conversations in a Time of Isolation

Take these words for those that I'll not write.
Take these words for everything we've said
and held in confidence. The page is white;
they'll have no part of us when we are dead.
Take them for the worries none will know,
spoken only that we might be free
of them, to say that someone, long ago,
was here to understand what troubled me
and I another. The fears need not survive:
they've had too much of us while we're alive
and what should not have been of you or me
will have no part of us in memory.

Take these for the words of solitude,
spoken when the world was held apart
in fear of unknown death, with gratitude
preserved beyond our years in careful art,
that someone understood what we were not
and spoke of what we never should have known
in order to transcend our earthly lot
and, reaching through our fears, not be alone.
Take these words for what you knew of me
and I of you, thankful and yet free
of their constraints: the troubles die unread;
they'll have no part of us when we are dead.

Take these for the words that none have said,
of criminals exhausted by their crimes
and those who would have loved as they had read
but fell asleep alone too many times,

for minds behind each wordless snout or beak
and all who'd speak but find no ear to tell:
the derelict and disregarded meek
who bow their heads and pray that all is well
and all oppressed by lawlessness or law
who had a dream of life and dream no more.
Take them for the words that won't be read;
they'll have no part of us when we are dead.

A Comedy Tonight

We declare a night of happiness
and drive all thoughts that trouble us away
by this decree. We assume the right,
so have as much authority as they.

We'll rule tonight as lords of revelry
and fill our courts with lovers, clowns and such
and lose ourselves in comedy and songs
and things we might regret, but not too much.

We'll have no words of worrying tonight
and when the dawn returns that we forget,
within the memory of what we did
the songs will rise and dancers pirouette.

Across the Hills to Home

Though shadows lurch as in a childhood tale
where night is full of mysteries and fear,
the moon is huge and gold above the hills
to light my way back home, and home draws near.

The moon is huge and gold above the hills
as if a god observed us and approved,
and suburbs twinkle like a land of dreams
as I drive home to rest where I am loved.

Encounters

A young cat wanders
through an afternoon
to find a family gathered
in their garden
in the sun…

What sadness is there
in this memory?

No more than in the sunlight
on your skin, or in the air
you breathe and feel you breathe
and know that you're alive
as they were then.

It's in the sun and air!
The moment's there,
and there they're happy, resting
on the grass
and playing as the sun
begins to sink,
beyond the touch of decades
yet to pass.

Babylonian Thought

This day you watch without enthusiasm
might, to future antiquarians,
seem lovely as a day in Babylon
with water sparkling in its broad canals.

And these unwanted chores would speak of life,
as if they were the errands of a scribe
who wandered high-walled streets, through skirted crowds,
as Shamash drew the sun across the heavens.

Cucumbers

Consider cucumbers. I have one here,
and slice it through its emerald skin
to smell the freshness, crisp and cool.
I cut it through again and hold

the slice towards a window, seeing
fibres in the glowing flesh
as if beneath a microscope,
with nutrients drawn from soil and sun,

and irrigation: nature and
humanity in harmony,
carried here across three thousand
years to burst between my teeth,

or slice in neat, white sandwiches,
or with tomatoes in a bowl
to eat when summer's at its height
and friends are gathered, yes, and laughing.

Mulberry

> When thou hearest the sound of a going in the tops
> of the mulberry trees, that then thou shalt bestir thyself:
> for then shall the Lord go out before thee, to smite
> the host of the Philistines.
> 2 Sam. 5:24

Mulberry leaves are gold about my head,
filled with summer light, or flecked with shade
of twigs and other leaves – shimmering gently
round the furrowed trunk that sinks beneath

the sand, its roots extending under grass
as moles and tiny insects tunnel and crawl
and nutrients are drawn towards the leaves
and drifting branches. Doves may settle there,

observing me, and squirrels scurry along
their dappled paths. The tree holds many worlds
beside its own, a multiplicity
on which to dream in search of understanding:

fruit will swell there, stained with lovers' blood,
and in the murmurs of the leaves and branches
you may hear the passage of your God
who moves ahead of you against your foes.

Supermarket Fruit Pot

I peel back a thin layer of film,
and there they sit, fresh and sweetly fragrant:
slices of papaya, single grapes,
and chunks of melon, glistening like jewels.

Suburban monarch, I select a piece
to crush between my teeth – watermelon
floods my mouth, sweet with sun and care,
then half a strawberry, and honeydew

as if from gardens built to rare design
to nourish fruits of all my spreading lands
and fruits of foreign travel, chilled with snow
and served on sunny days for my delight.

To Attar's Nightingale

> Don't presume the road is short. Many oceans
> and deserts lie between the Beloved and us.
> 'The Hoopoe', *The Conference of the Birds*,
> ATTAR OF NISHAPUR, translated by Sholeh Wolpé

Nightingale, wait – don't take this path
through suffering to silence. Turn and fly,
fly swiftly to your rose. She waits for you;
she trembles in her garden for your song.
You have your wisdom: call the coral colours
from her depths - flutter gracefully
amid the thorns that guard her from the world
and tell her of her beauty. She's alone.
Be brave and comfort her as petals fade
although the winds are soft and sunlight gentle
in the garden – sing as when you sang
and she awoke, her sepals damp with dew,
and sing of colours none but you would find
so she will know them, casting piping notes
across the towns, across the listening land,
where they will come to rest, as soft as feathers.

Tourist Bus, Long Street

The bus rolls slowly through the city traffic,
passing ageing buildings and the crowds
to cross the mountains, green and gold with summer,
circling back along the sparkling sea

as occupants snap photos, sunlit on
the open upper deck, and gesturing
to sights that they'll remember when they're home,
of life where life was hidden from the world,

and those they pass, while busy with their days,
might wonder for a moment what they see,
of life that's lived amid a history
beneath the brilliance of a southern sun

in which to holiday – the bus rolls on,
between car guards directing cars in place
beneath the craggy mountains, to the sea,
and life is seen and worthy to be seen.

Ducks in a Garden, Cape Town

> Your seeing changes everything
> 'Picking Oranges', DOUGLAS REID SKINNER

Ducks are rootling grass still damp with dew
as sunlight glows from a cloudless sky,
gleaming on the leaves of cup-of-gold
that tremble round a false acacia's frame.

I play no part – but this would not have been
were I not here to glimpse the peaceful scene.

I watch them pace beside a garden wall,
busy in their vivid, tactile world
beneath hibiscus, open to the sun,
as morning's chatter drifts among the trees.

I play no part – but this would not have been
were I not here to glimpse the peaceful scene.

Revolutions

A goose stands one-legged on a chimney,
head on breast beside a gibbous moon
of ghostly white in blue and golden light
as earth revolves to noon.

There's no sadness here among the roofs
or in the light and shadow of the trees
beneath a moon beside a goose that stands,
unmoving as a frieze

where figures dance as if their world endured
and they might pass beneath a gibbous moon
of ghostly white in blue and golden light
as earth revolves to noon.

Into Town

~ Nelson Mandela Boulevard, Cape Town

A line of palms divides the motorway
and when it's windy, and the sun is bright,
the palm fronds buck and sway and catch the light
like waves that glimmer in the wind-blown bay

or plastic shaped to somebody's design
in buildings that appear as cars descend
towards the town, around the mountain bend
and down, past fronds that change as if a sign

that what awaits is not what lies behind
and drivers' spirits lift. Not knowing why,
they feel the promises of days gone by
when they might travel into town to find

a holiday's amusement with their friends,
or glimpse a time when such a thing might be,
that here between the mountains and the sea
their lives might yet be turned to other ends.
Palm fronds buck and sway and catch the light;
the day is windy, and the sun is bright.

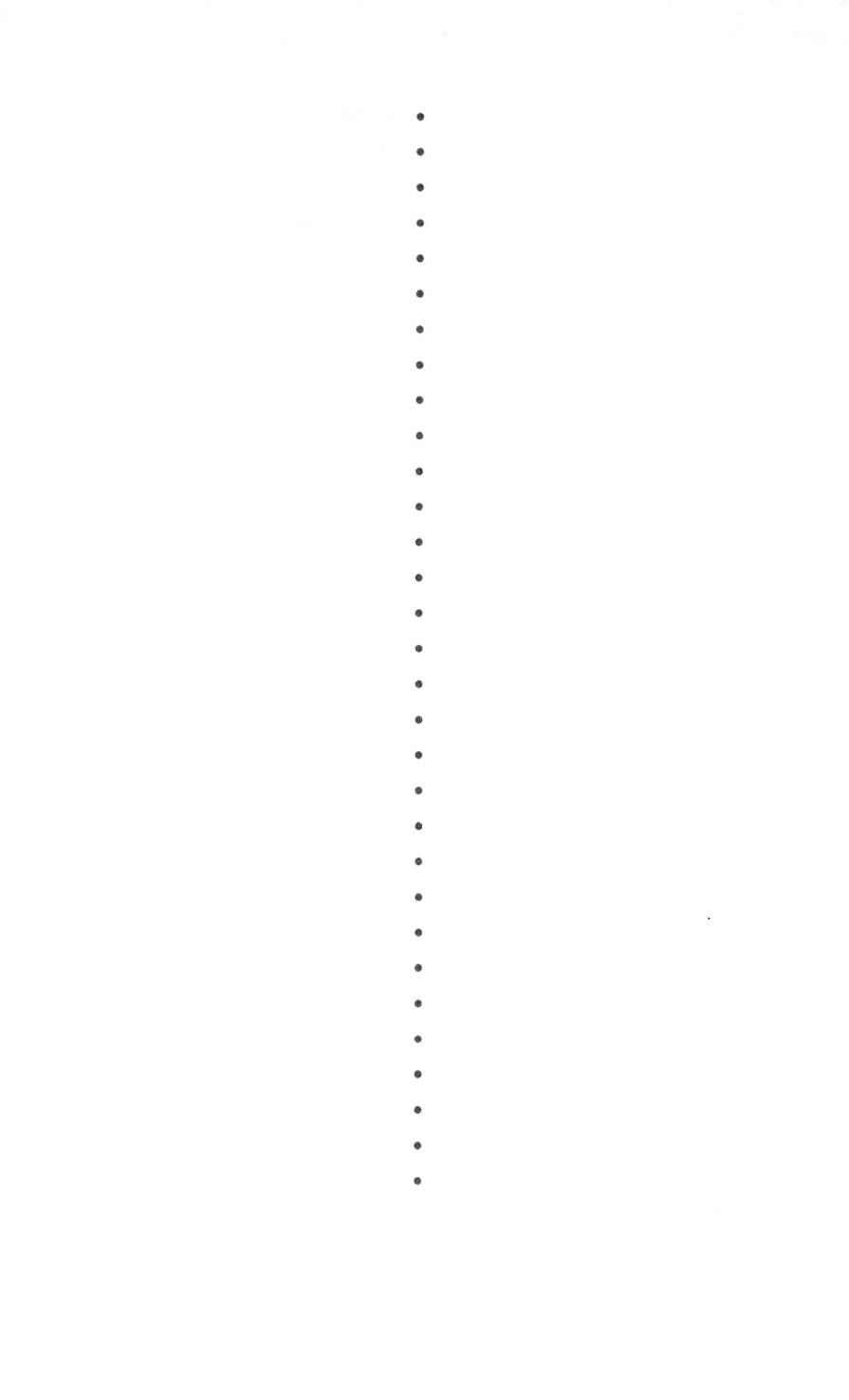

NOTES ON THE POEMS

p9 The quotation is taken from the CK Scott Montcrieff translation of Marcel Proust's *La Prisonnière* as *The Captive*, chapter 1.

p11 David Attenborough, quoted in *The Guardian*, 21 October 2011.

p19 Adapted from the first letter of Héloïse to Abelard. *The Letter and Other Writings*, William Levitan et al.

p20 With thanks to the New York Dolls.

p21 *Samuel Taylor Coleridge: Selected Poems* (Edited with an Introduction and Notes by Richard Holmes).

p26 Aias or Ajax is a mythological hero, the son of King Telamon and Periboea. He plays an important role in the Trojan War, and is mainly known as a warrior of great courage in Homer's *Iliad* and the eponymous play by Sophocles. 'Light and Darkness in Sophocles' Ajax', WB Stanford, 1978.

p27 Quoted in *The Dead Will Arise: Nongqawuse and the Great Cattle-Killing of 1856–7*, Jeff Peires.

p39 From 'An apology for Raymond Sebond', Michel de Montaigne, *The Complete Essays*, trans. by MA Screech.

p53 Regarding the Proust quote, see the Note above for p9.

p55 – Dia!kwain was one of the chief contributors to the archive of Bushman literature and languages collected and translated by Wilhelm Bleek and Lucy Lloyd in Mowbray, Cape Town (Bleek and Lloyd Collection, University of Cape Town). His contributions were in the |Xam language.
– 'the water-bull'. 'Mother used to say that the water's people are accustomed to pull out the water's bull ['cow' is crossed out] from the water, that they may lead him away, that they may go (and) killing him lay him down (upon) ['at' is inserted above 'upon'] their land/ground ['land' is added above 'ground'].' The note 'The Bushmen's place' is added on the facing page. – Lucy Lloyd's translation, notebook V–3.

p58 "the *taifa* left unconquered". A *taifa* was an independent Muslim principality of Al-Andalus.

p59 Part of the Seikilos epitaph, an inscription on the Seikilos stele.

Free translation from the Greek by Thomas J Mathiesen in *Apollo's Lyre: Greek Music and Music Theory in Antiquity and the Middle Ages*. The stele (from the city of Tralleis near the modern city of Aydın, Turkey) is usually regarded as having been raised by Seikilos for his wife Euterpe, although there are other interpretations.

p62 The image *Yusuf tends his flock* has been attributed to the painter Muhammadi ('The Age of Muhammadi', Soudavar Abolala, in *Muqarnas: An Annual on the Visual Culture of the Islamic World, XVII*).

p65 Praxilla was a Greek poet of the 5th century BCE. The quote is from one of the surviving fragments of poetry, 'Hymn to Adonis'. The words are spoken by Adonis in the underworld. From *Greek Lyric Poets* by Francis Brooks.

p67 The reign of Diocletian marks the end of the Crisis of the Third Century and the move from the Principate to the Dominate.

p71 The title is taken from the film *A Funny Thing Happened on the Way to the Forum*.

p76 '… stained with lovers' blood …' Pyramus and Thisbe were a pair of ill-fated Babylonian lovers whose story is told in Ovid's *Metamorphoses*. It is thought the story is of Cilician origin.

p78 *The Conference of the Birds* by Attar, translated by Sholeh Wolpé.

p80 'Picking Oranges', *The House in Pella District*, Douglas Reid Skinner.

NOTES ON THE AUTHOR

STUART PAYNE's first volume of poetry, *Voices from Another Room,* was published in 2018 by Crane River. In 2019, he had two poems commissioned by the AVBOB Poetry Competition and in 2022 his poem 'Words for Dia!kwain' won the National Poetry Prize. He handles obituaries and research at *Stanzas* and is currently one of the hosts of the Off the Wall poetry group.